Taking the Bodhisattva Vow

D0205132

Immanent nature of samsara and nirvana
the clear light.
The saintly Dharma shows the mode of being
the clear light.
May the fortunate ones who practice
the mahamudra-clear light
become Buddhas in the heart of Awakening
the clear light
BOKAR RINPOCHE

Publisher's Acknowledgement

The publisher gratefully acknowledges the generous help of Jason Espada, Rosemary Gilpin, Karen Graham, Michael DeNoya, Elson Snow, Carolyn Sumrall, Isao and Sets Tanaka.

Cover drawing by Carolyn Sumrall.

Taking the Bodhisattva Vow

Bokar Rinpoche

Translation from French into English
Christiane Buchet

ClearPoint Press
San Francisco, California

Taking the Bodhisattva Vow

Published by:
ClearPoint Press
PO Box 170658
San Francisco, CA 94117

The original text of this book was published in French and was titled **Le vœu de Bodhisattva**. Copyright reserved for all countries: Association Claire Lumière, Mas Vinsargues, 13116 Vernègues, France.

Copyright © 1997 English Edition
ClearPoint Press
Printed in the United States of America
Printed on acid-free paper
Library of Congress Catalog Card Number:
97-77053

Table of contents

Presentation

About the Text

Buddhism offers several perspectives, that each have various theories, methods of practice, and commitments. The most common division is that of three vehicles, each with a particular objective and vows.

- The **Small Vehicle** *(Hinayana)* leads the practitioner to liberation from samsara in an individual perspective. The vows, called "vows of individual liberation," are related to the Small Vehicle, that is, the various vows of monks or nuns (minor ordination and major ordination) and the vows of lay practitioners.

- The **Great Vehicle** *(Mahayana)* has the goal of obtaining full Awakening, the perfect Buddhahood, not in order to attain personal happiness but to gain the skills necessary to guide all beings to the cessation of suffering; the Bodhisattva vow is related to it.

- The **Diamond Vehicle** *(Vajrayana)* appears as a branch of the Great Vehicle. Its goal is identical, and its distinctive feature is that it makes use of methods well known for accomplishing results quickly. Many sacred commitments, called *samayas*, are contained in it.

The purpose of this work is to present a clear exposition of the vow inherent in the second of these vehicles, the Mahayana. Many people have heard of the Bodhisattva vow; indeed, they have actually taken the vow, but have remained uncertain as to its exact nature and implications. Here, we will find precise answers to such questions as: what is a Bodhisattva; what is the Bodhicitta; what are the commitments of taking the vow; who may take it; how does the ceremony unfold; which precepts follow the vow; how does one purify transgression of the vow; and so on.

The teachings transcribed here were given by Bokar Rinpoche in Bodhgaya in November 1995, during a seminar of study and meditation intended for Westerners. Some of these teachings were delivered during a long ceremony of taking the Bodhisattva vow, which occurred under the foliage of the Bodhi Tree, where the Buddha attained Awakening. Others are the results of private interviews.

Bokar Rinpoche referred to several texts in delivering this teaching.

- *The Jewel Ornament of Liberation (Dhakpo Thargyen)* by Gampopa
- *The Embellishment of Lapis-lazuli (Bedurya tratsom)* by Khenpo Lodro Donyo, a commentary upon the preceding text, explaining that which is presented allusively or incidentally in Gampopa's text
- *The Treasury of All Knowledge, (Sheja zo)* by Jamgon Lodro Taye, which notably clarifies the transgressions
- *A Guide to the Bodhisattva's Way of Life (Bhodhisattvacharyavatara)* by Shantideva, the fundamental text illustrating the way of the Bodhisattva

About the Author

Bokar Rinpoche was born in Tibet in the year of the Iron Dragon (1940) into a nomadic family of horse, yak, goat, and sheep breeders.

He was four years old when His Holiness Karmapa the Sixteenth, head of the Kagyupa school, recognized him as a *tulku*—reincarnation of the previous Bokar Rinpoche. Educated first at the monastery founded by his previous reincarnation, he pursued his training in Tsurphu, the seat of the Karmapas. At a very young age, he took charge of the Bokar community in Western Tibet, not far from Mount Kailash, which is one of the most important sacred places of Hinduism and Buddhism.

The Chinese invasion caused him to go into exile when he was in his twenties. After many hardships, he was able, with those who chose to follow him, to reach Mustang in Northern Nepal, and then India.

In India he met Kalu Rinpoche. He became Kalu Rinpoche's chief disciple, and was called to succeed him as the head of the Shangpa Kagyu lineage—one of the eight great original lineages through which Buddhism went from India to Tibet.

Bokar Rinpoche twice accomplished the traditional three-year and three-month retreat in Sonada, the Indian monastery of Kalu Rinpoche located not far from Darjeeling.

Bokar Rinpoche's remarkable qualities caused him to be chosen by Kalu Rinpoche to direct the retreat centers in Sonada, and by His Holiness the Sixteenth Karmapa to take charge of the retreat center of Rumtek, the new seat of the Karmapas in Sikkim, an Indian territory between Nepal and Bhutan. In Mirik, Bokar Rinpoche also founded a monastery and retreat center dedicated to Kalachakra practice. Those duties make him one of the main masters of meditation of the Kagyupa school.

Bokar Rinpoche takes great care in the preservation and transmission of the Buddha's teachings in our difficult and troubled time. He strives to do so in three areas:

- for exiled Tibetans, by directing studies and practice in his monastery in Mirik and by helping, as much as possible, the monasteries of Sonada and Rumtek.
- for the Tibetans in Tibet, by reconstructing his monastery in Bokar, ordaining monks, and starting a retreat center.
- for Westerners, by each winter conducting a seminar of apprenticeship for meditation especially designed for them.

— François Jacquemart

PART ONE

The Vow

1- Nature of the Vow

Since time without beginning, because we habitually function in a mode of an "I" cherishing itself, we continually search for what is good, pleasant, and beautiful for ourselves. We search for our own happiness, and we are really not concerned about bringing what is good, pleasant, and beautiful to others.

However, we must understand that from the viewpoint of their aspirations, all beings are equal to ourselves. All want happiness as much as we want it; all try to avoid suffering as much as we do.

If we think about it, what is the personal space we occupy? Quantitatively, we represent a single individual, whereas others represent an infinite number of individuals. Others being much more important than ourselves, we must generate an attitude that includes the wish that they find happiness and avoid suffering, and nourish our own will to help them in this quest. It is from this perspective that the vow can be found.

Nature of the Bodhisattva Vow

What is the nature of the Bodhisattva vow? It is the commitment, formulated as follows: "To lead others to happiness and to liberate them from suffering, I will attain Awakening. Such is the promise I make today."

We want to attain Awakening, and the reason we want to attain it is to benefit all beings.

Making this promise, we follow the same path followed by the previous Buddhas. This is why we take the vow in reference to them, thinking:

"Just as the Buddhas of the past, when they were still ordinary beings, first have taken the commitment to attain Buddhahood for benefiting all beings; just as they have continued on the path of the Bodhisattva, practicing the six paramitas up to the perfection; and just as they have attained Buddhahood; in the same way, following their example, I also will realize Buddhahood for the benefit of all beings."

As told by Shantideva in the *Guide to the Bodhisattva's Way of Life*, "Just as the previous Buddhas gave rise to the thought of Awakening and have trained little by little, I generate in myself the thought of Awakening for the benefit of the world and I will practice all the preparatory exercises in their order."

> To lead others to happiness
> and to free them from suffering,
> I will attain Awakening.
> Such is the promise I make today.

Three essential ideas are included in this promise:
- the aim to benefit all beings by attaining Buddhahood
- I make this my aim
- the means to attain this aim is the practice of the six paramitas

The importance of this promise is demonstrated by the fact that its utterance is witnessed by the Buddhas and Bodhisattvas of the ten directions.

Definition of the Term Bodhisattva Vow

The Bodhisattva vow embodies the realization of the motivation of the Great Vehicle. Its exact appellation is the *Bodhicitta vow*, that is, the vow of Awakening which in Tibetan is *jang chub gy sem gy dompa*. The following is an explanation.

-*jang chub* translates the Sanskrit term *bodhi*; this means Awakening and brings out two ideas. *Jang* means "purified," that is, entirely purified from the veil of the conflicting emotions and the veil of the objects of knowledge. *Chub* means "perfected" and refers to the perfect possession of qualities, notably the omniscience that knows the ultimate nature of all phenomena and their manifestation. The term Awakening is synonymous with Buddhahood.

- *gy* means "of"
- *sem* (Sanskrit, *citta*) means "mind," the mind as cause, the foundation of obtaining the qualities of Buddhahood; Awakening is not separated from mind.
- *dompa*, means "vow" and here designates the commitment or the promise to attain Awakening.

བྱང་ཆུབ་ཀྱི་སེམས་ཀྱི་སྡོམ་པ

Jang chub gy sem gy dompa

Vow of the Awakened Mind

Therefore, the Bodhisattva vow is the "promise to [realize] the Awakened mind" or the "promise to [lead] the mind to Awakening."

The motivation of this promise—which is the will to liberate all beings from suffering—is understood in this phrase.

Subdivisions of Bodhicitta

Several classifications are used to describe the various aspects of Bodhicitta.

The first classification lists 22 stages of Bodhicitta, from the beginner's level to Buddhahood. These 22 stages of Bodhicitta are divided into four categories, based on the stages of the Bodhisattva.

- The Bodhicitta of ordinary beings, those who have not attained the Bodhisattva's stages
- The Bodhicitta of the Bodhisattvas from the first to the seventh stage
- The Bodhicitta of the Bodhisattvas from the eighth to the tenth stage (pure stages)
- The Bodhicitta of Buddhahood

Aside from these classifications that apply to progression, the main division of Bodhicitta, in terms of its nature, considers two aspects, absolute and relative Bodhicitta.

ABSOLUTE BODHICITTA, designating the nature of the mind itself, is the union of emptiness and compassion, the mind itself, beyond all concepts such as existence and nonexistence.

RELATIVE BODHICITTA is the mind moved by great compassion that turns itself toward beings and thinks, "I must liberate all beings from the suffering of samsara and establish them in

Buddhahood. It is absolutely necessary that I liberate them." It is a thought of love and concern.

Relative Bodhicitta itself is made of two phases, ASPIRING BODHICITTA and REALIZING BODHICITTA. These are envisioned in slightly different ways in various traditions.

In the tradition of the Profound View of Nagarjuna, the thought, "I will attain Buddhahood to benefit all beings," is aspiring Bodhicitta. Then acting on this thought, that is, treading the path leading to Awakening, constitutes realizing Bodhicitta. To make a comparison, the thought of "I want to go to Bodhgaya" is the equivalent of aspiring Bodhicitta whereas treading the path that actually leads to Bodhgaya corresponds to realizing Bodhicitta.

In the tradition of the Vast Action of Asanga, the thought, "I will commit myself to attaining Buddhahood for the benefit of all beings," the reference to the goal (Buddhahood) constitutes aspiring Bodhicitta. Then, the thought "I commit to put into practice the means to attain this goal" (that is, the six paramitas), which refers to the cause that allows us to attain the result, constitutes realizing Bodhicitta. In this case, to follow the previous comparison, the decision to go to Bodhgaya is still aspiring Bodhicitta, however, realizing Bodhicitta, is not actually treading the path, but rather a second decision to begin treading the path with the understanding that the goal cannot otherwise be attained.

In the tradition of Nagarjuna, realizing Bodhicitta refers therefore to the actual practicing of the means, whereas in the tradition of Asanga, it refers to the commitment to put them into practice. The first of these two traditions distinguishes aspiring from realizing, whereas the latter distinguishes aspiration for the goal from aspiration for the means.

Importance of Bodhicitta
The Buddha's teaching can be divided in various ways. Here is the classification into three baskets (tripitaka)—the sutras, vinaya, and abhidharma—or the classification according to the perspective of individual liberation (Small Vehicle), of the vehicle of the Bodhisattvas (Great Vehicle), and of the Vajrayana (tantras).

In the second type of classification, we encounter three kinds of ethic: the ethic of individual liberation, the Bodhisattva vow, and the commitments inherent to Vajrayana empowerments. The ethic of individual liberation, which includes the vows of a monk (or a nun) and the vows of the layperson, aims at avoiding all that is harmful to ourselves—mostly in the activity of the body and speech. Of course, there are also rules about the mind, but they are not as important.

The Bodhisattva vow inherent to the Great Vehicle places greater importance on the mind, without neglecting activity of body and speech. Moreover, its intention is less to protect oneself than to benefit others. The foundation of this vow is love and compassion.

As for Vajrayana commitments, they are not located in the mind as psyche but are found at the level of primordial knowledge (*jnana*).

In this way, we approach more subtle levels. Finally, when we attain the nature of mind itself, as it is, this is Buddhahood.

The Bodhisattva vow and the precepts associated with it play an important role in this progression. Without them, it is impossible to reach Buddhahood.

The force of Bodhicitta is immense. If the mind has it, body and speech will also spontaneously adopt positive conduct and will shun negative acts naturally. When Bodhicitta is really integrated into our mind, its effects will not be limited to our present life. We will find its power again in our dreams and future lives, where love and compassion and the wish to help others remain with us.

Countless benefits flow from Bodhicitta. As stated in the *Guide to the Bodhisattva's Way of Life* by Shantideva:

When the mind embraces the constant thought of liberating the unlimited number of beings, it sometimes falls asleep or may be dissipated but the flow of its merits become unceasingly greater, like the infinity of space.

Who May Take the Vow?

To take the Bodhisattva vow, it is not sufficient to have a precious human existence. It is also necessary to belong to the Mahayana family, which is defined as a natural inclination for peace, love, and compassion, and by spontaneous attraction and immediate confidence in the Mahayana teachings.

We must also take refuge in the Three Jewels and place ourselves under the protection of the Buddha, Dharma, and Sangha. This taking refuge must be placed in the perspective of the Great Vehicle and include the following elements.

- concerning duration, we take refuge not only in this lifetime but from now until we attain Awakening

- concerning the person, we do not consider taking refuge alone, but that the infinity of beings of the universe take refuge at the same time as we do

- concerning the motivation, we take refuge to liberate the infinite number of beings from the endless sufferings of samsara and to establish them all in perfect happiness of Awakening

Asanga's tradition of the Vast Action insists, furthermore, on the importance of having taken some vows of individual liberation (lay practitioner vows, minor and major ordination) to receive the Bodhisattva vow. In Nagarjuna's tradition of the Profound View, it is said that it is sufficient to renounce negative acts and observe correct ethic. To take the Bodhisattva vow, it is therefore not only necessary to avoid all that is harmful to others in the activity of our body, speech, and mind, we must also strive to accomplish what is beneficial for others, whether or not we have taken the vows of individual liberation.

Being Ready to Take the Vow
Some people hesitate to take the Bodhisattva vow, thinking that it demands qualities they lack. Their feelings of love and compassion are neither strong nor great. The wish to harm and harboring negative thoughts toward others have not left their minds.

How can we know if we are ready to take the Bodhisattva vow?

If we greatly value love and compassion, if we see their benefits—made apparent to us by listening to teachings—if we consider that ill-will, anger, and hatred are defects, we are ready. We must take the vow. The vow helps us improve. It will be useless for a person who has no ill-will, who is good by nature, or who is not stained by conflicting emotions to take the vow. We take the vow precisely because we recognize the presence of ill-will and conflicting emotions that we want to eliminate within ourselves. The more anger and aversion we see within ourselves, the more we must be determined to take the Bodhisattva vow.

The Master's Presence

Some people believe that the individual intention to develop love and the determination to attain Awakening for the benefit of all are sufficient forces; they think that taking the vow will add nothing. However, the vow has inherent benefits, and this considerably reinforces individual determination. This power derives from the fact that in the ceremony, we solemnly make the promise of attaining Awakening for benefiting all beings, with all Buddhas and Bodhisattvas as witnesses.

Our mind is strongly imprinted with the magnitude and importance of the commitment. Even if some ill-will persists in our mind, we will be more inclined to reject it because we will remember our promise. The power of this commitment is sufficient to continue through our future lives.

The power of this vow is increased by the fact that it is taken in front of a master. We can take the Bodhisattva vow in front of the Bodhi tree, for instance, or simply imagine the presence of the Buddhas and Bodhisattvas in the sky without anyone actually present. The vow has the same validity whether or not it is taken in the presence of a master. However, it is not imprinted in us with the same force that it has with the memory of the master, a human person, easily and vividly imposed on our mind. The thought, "It is in front of my master that I have taken the Bodhisattva vow," will help us not to act contrary to our commitment. We will think of him or her more easily than of the Bodhi tree or of a Buddha whose presence we may have imagined.

Briefly, for the imperfect beings that we are, wishing as we do to tread the path of Awakening, taking the Bodhisattva vow can only benefit us. Shantideva underlines this by composing a eulogy of Bodhicitta.

It is an elixir to abolish death in the world, an inexhaustible treasure to eliminate all misery in the world, an incomparable remedy to heal the sickness of the world, a tree to shelter the world tired of wandering on the path of life, a bridge open to lead out of painful ways, a spiritual moon rising to cool the burning of worldly passions, a great sun to dissipate darkness of ignorance, a new butter produced by churning the genuine milk of the Dharma.

For the human caravan, following the road of life and hungry for happiness, there is a feast of happiness where all the coming beings will be satiated.

Nagarjuna lived between 150 and 200 C.E. A scholar and greatly accomplished master, he founded the Madhyamika school and wrote voluminous treatises. He originated one of the two great lineages of the Bodhisattva vow, that of the Profound View received from Manjushri.

2- The Bodhisattva

The Bodhisattva is represented in the Mahayana as the ideal practitioner of the spiritual path leading to authentic Awakening. Awakening is both complete understanding of the ultimate nature of all phenomena and universal equanimous compassion.

The word "Bodhisattva" refers, however, to three different kinds of beings. Differentiation between these three is needed to avoid confusion. There are:
- apprentice Bodhisattvas
- Bodhisattvas in the stages
- Bodhisattvas as emanations of the Buddhas

Apprentice Bodhisattvas
In some ways, any individual who has taken the Bodhisattva vow is a Bodhisattva. This person actually has the motivation inherent into the Bodhisattva (that is, attaining Awakening for the benefit of all beings). He or she has uttered the formal promise to attain his or her goal, and practices according to his or her capabilities to attain this goal.

However, we cannot really say that this person is a Bodhisattva, if a sufficient level of spiritual development has not been attained. He or she is not liberated from samsara or conflicting emotions; he or she does not have the vision of the true nature of everything; he or she can benefit beings only on a small scale. This individual is more in the situation of a medical student than in the situation of someone who, having successfully completed his or her medical studies, can practice medicine effectively.

This is why, although one may use the name of Bodhisattva for any person who has taken the Bodhisattva vow, it would better to talk of an apprentice Bodhisattva or of a member of the Bodhisattva family.

Stages of the Bodhisattvas
A true Bodhisattva is a being who has attained one of the ten Bodhisattva stages. It is to this being that the term Bodhisattva is applicable.

Having attained the first Bodhisattva stage means that, by practicing the two Bodhicittas, relative and absolute, we arrive at a direct vision of what was not previously seen, the mode of being of the mind, the reality of the nature in itself. This stage is also the stage of having attained liberation out of samsara and never falling into it again. Not seeing or seeing this reality is the dividing line between ordinary beings and those who have attained the first stage. The development of this vision and a lessening of the veils covering the mind permit the progression from the first to the tenth Bodhisattva stage. The vision of the mode of being of the mind is stable on the first stage, however, it does not have the same sharpness while the individual is meditating or in nonmeditative states.

From the first to the tenth stages, a progressive development of the qualities inherent to Bodhisattvahood unfolds. It is similar to the increasing light of the moon while waxing. It is only with Buddhahood occurring after the tenth stage, that the mind, purified of all imperfections, attains the wholeness of its qualities.

It is sometimes said that the Bodhisattva ideal would be to stop the progression toward Buddhahood to continue working for the benefit of all beings in samsara. This affirmation is founded on some confusion. First, it is necessary to understand that the Bodhisattva, even if working in samsara, does not belong to samsara. On the first stage, the Bodhisattva is liberated. Secondly, it is erroneous to believe that the faculties possessed by a Bodhisattva to help beings are superior to those of a Buddha, because the qualities of a Buddha are infinite. The aim of a Bodhisattva is, therefore, not to put a halt on the way to Buddhahood, thinking it would help beings if he or she stays in the Bodhisattva stages, but to attain Buddhahood.

Bodhisattvas as Emanations of Buddhas
The confusion as to the objectives of the Bodhisattva is mainly a question of vocabulary. When it is affirmed that a Bodhisattva benefits beings, whereas a Buddha does not, it appears that the term *Buddha* is limited in this case to the Absolute Body (Dharmakaya) and that the form Bodies, the Body of Enjoyment (Sambhogakaya) and the Body of Emanation (Nirmanakaya) only receive the title of *Bodhisattva.* As it is true that it is not the Dharmakaya of a Buddha that accomplishes the benefit of beings, but indeed the Sambhogakaya and Nirmanakaya, then according to this point of view, it is indeed the *Bodhisattva* who is in charge of benefiting beings.

In reality, however, a Buddha possesses the three Bodies and consequently has the ability to help beings in various ways, including the manifestation of a Bodhisattva.

This ability is why many Bodhisattvas are not beings working on the levels of the Bodhisattva stages but are emanations of Buddhas. The Buddha manifests a body, divine or human, whose aspect is a Bodhisattva, although essentially remaining a Buddha.

These Bodhisattvas are emanations of Buddhas and manifest themselves in two modes corresponding to the formal Bodies:
- under divine form, that of the Sambhogakaya as Avalokiteshvara, Manjushri, Vajrapani, and many others for the beings with pure karma
- under human or another form for ordinary beings

Therefore, we generally differentiate between the two types of Bodhisattvas, those who are in the Bodhisattva stages and on the way to Buddhahood and those who are emanations of Buddhas.

The Bodhisattva vow concerns above all the Bodhisattvas in the stages and even more the apprentice Bodhisattvas.

The meaning of the Word
Breaking down the noun *jangchub sempa*, which translates the Sanskrit term Bodhisattva into Tibetan, allows us to see its meaning with precision.
- *jangchub* means Awakening and is synonymous with perfect and unsurpassable Buddhahood
- *sempa* means courageous mind

The Bodhisattva, therefore, is one whose mind turns with courage to Awakening. Why this idea of courage? For three reasons: duration, magnitude, and difficulty of the task.

Bodhisattva Avalokiteshvara

A Bodhisattva, first, does not assign to himself or herself a short-term task, but a task that spreads over many *kalpas*.

Secondly, the Bodhisattva commitment is not limited to the willingness to help a determined number of beings but is concerned with the totality of beings.

Thirdly, the Bodhisattva is ready to fearlessly face all difficulties included in the practice of generosity, ethic, patience, and other paramitas.

Activity of the Bodhisattvas
The activity of the Bodhisattvas is extremely varied, vast, and profound, according to the needs and aspirations of beings. Bodhisattvas teach the Dharma to those who need it, strive to provide food to those who are hungry, clothes to those who are naked, and remedies to those who are ill. Bodhisattvas can, if necessary, take the form of an animal. They can also create conditions necessary for building bridges, ships, houses, and so on, searching with wisdom and compassion to relieve suffering of beings everywhere. As Shantideva poetically said:

> *May I be the protector of abandoned beings, a guide for those who tread the path, and for those who wish to cross, may I be a boat, the road, the bridge; may I be the lamp for those who need a lamp, the bed for*

those who need a bed, the slave for those who need a slave, the miraculous stone, the horn of abundance, the magic formula, the plant that heals, the wish-filling tree, the cow of wishes.

The Four Activities
Bodhisattvas and Buddhas put into effect the four types of Awakened activity to materially and spiritually assist beings.
- PACIFYING, which has the goal of relieving beings of their actual suffering and to dissipate conflicting emotions that cause such suffering.
- INCREASING, which allows the development of well-being, richness, merit and spiritual realizations.
- POWER, by which Bodhisattva can exert beneficial action on a large scale.
- WRATHFUL ACTIVITY, which when revealed to be necessary in some cases, can be used out of compassion and in well-defined circumstances.

Kalu Rinpoche, in a dedication prayer called *The Great Vessel of Liberation*, summarizes the Bodhisattva wishes for putting into effect the four Awakened activities.

May I dissipate all illness and suffering of beings by the power and dedication just as the Buddha has done.

May life, merit, power, mastery, experiences, and realizations increase as a river at the end of the rainy season.

In order to bring sublime benefit to the Doctrine and to all beings
May I gather under my power the three spheres and the three worlds.

In order to have the capabilities to liberate the enemies who made up the 'ten fields,'
May the efficiency and force of the wrathful mantras shine like a fire.

Wrathful Activity

If the first kinds of activity mentioned above are easy to understand, the last one is less clear. We must understand, however, that wrathful activity is to be used with compassion for the benefit of all, when the other modes of action fail to modify the conduct of individuals whose acts are extremely harmful to others and themselves, leading them to birth into hell and intolerable suffering.

Wrathful activity is the working of compassion since it protects those who are victims of negative acts as much as their authors. It prevents the latter from creating new causes for suffering. This activity can even suppress life, but a Bodhisattva act must meet the following conditions:

- The one who acts must not feel any anger, animosity, or aggressiveness against the being to be killed.
- He or she must feel, on the contrary, infinite compassion for this being.
- He or she must have as the only motivation to prevent this being future suffering as a consequence of these negative acts.
- He or she must end life not with weapons or poisons, but by the power of mantras.

The Navigator Great Compassion

The *Jatakas* (tales of former lives of the Buddha) illustrate this activity. The future Buddha, then a Bodhisattva, was born as a merchant navigator whose name was Great Compassion (Depon Nyingje Chenpo). One day, Great Compassion was caring for 500 merchants on his ship. A bandit named Black Man with a Stick also embarked. His plan was to kill the merchants and take their goods. Great Compassion, who could read thoughts, knew the intention of Black Man with a Stick. He also knew that the 500 merchants were, in fact, 500 Bodhisattvas. He thought, "If this bandit kills the 500 Bodhisattvas, he will accumulate negative karma so severe that he will suffer for numberless kalpas."

To immediately protect the merchants and to protect the bandit from future suffering, Great Compassion killed Black Man with a Stick.

It is said that for this act, far from being negative, Great Compassion earned the equivalent of many kalpas of accumulation of merit.

The navigator Great Compassion prevents
Black Man with a Stick from carrying out his misdeed.

3- Buddha and Bodhicitta

Buddha Shakyamuni, like all the Buddhas, was at first an ordinary being. Like all Buddhas, he first engendered Bodhicitta, then, for many lives continued on the path leading him to final Awakening.

Several stories tell how, during his past lives, he turned his mind to Awakening, taking in a formal or informal way the Bodhisattva vow. Some of the stories presented here are classified within the framework of the Small Vehicle or Great Vehicle, respectively.

According to the Small Vehicle
The Story of Offering Soup
Many kalpas ago, Shakya Tupten Buddha was living on Earth. The future Buddha came in his presence and gave him a clay cup decorated with a mirror and filled with soup. The future Buddha told him, "Blessed One, may I be like you in the future in every way; having the same disciples, same life span, same activity, and same field of activity."

From that time on the future Buddha took up the Bodhisattva conduct.

King Most Luminous and the Furious Elephant
The future Buddha was born as the King Most Luminous (Sanskrit, *Tisya;* Tibetan, *Rabtsal*). The king possessed a magnificent white elephant whose taming he entrusted to one of his servants. The servant applied himself for long months and returned when he thought the animal was tamed. The king wanted to try riding right away and got on the back of the elephant. Joined by his court, he went into the forest. Unfortunately, the white elephant scented a female elephant. Seized by desire, the elephant ran wildly after the one who excited his senses. Terrified, the king saved himself only by grasping a branch, leaving his mount to continue his reckless course.

Back in the palace, the king called his servant to severely reprimand him, "You have presented me with the elephant, pretending to have tamed him. However, the elephant ran off in the forest, and my life was saved only by a branch."

"Your Majesty," answered the servant, "it is not that I have not accomplished my work correctly. I tamed the body of the elephant, but taming his mind is not in my power. In this world, only the Buddha can tame minds."

King Most Luminous grabbed branches to save his life.

When the king heard the word "Buddha," a great feeling of faith was born in his mind. He went immediately to the Buddha who was living on Earth, and in the Buddha's presence, vowed to dedicate himself to attain Awakening.

The Future Buddha Released from Hell
The future Buddha at one time was an ordinary being, who, by the power of his negative acts, was born into hell. Along with another unfortunate companion, he had to unceasingly pull a heavy cart. The future Buddha had some strength, but his companion was really weak and struggled to pull his load. His companion was often struck with a stick by the guard who was watching them. In the mind of the future Buddha arose great compassion for his suffering companion. Turning to the guard, he made a plea for pity, "My companion is weak and I am strong. Allow me to pull the cart. Do not bear down on him." These words only had the effect of provoking terrible anger in the guard. The guard raised his stick and violently hit the future Buddha's head, leaving him dead.

When the future Buddha regained consciousness, he was no longer in hell but in the realm of gods, where his mind turned to Awakening.

Ocean Dust Similar to the White Lotus

In the Great Vehicle, the main story of the conversion of the future Buddha who was searching for Awakening is as follows:

Having taken birth as a Brahman called Ocean Dust (Gyamtso'dul), the future Buddha was one of a thousand princes, each to become one of a thousand Buddhas of our kalpa.

In the presence of their father, the Buddha Quintessence of Jewels (Rinchen Nyingpo), the princes envisioned how they would attain Awakening for the benefit of all beings in different ways. One promised to become a Buddha and work for the benefit of all when the human life span on Earth would be 80,000 years; another, when it would be 40,000 years; another when it would be 20,000 years, and so on. Each chose a particular time in the future kalpa.

However, no prince would select the period when human beings would live 100 years (that is, our actual life span). The future Buddha asked his brothers, "None of you wants to guide human beings when they live to be 100 years old?" "No, the task is too difficult," they answered. "Human beings will then be resisting any teaching. They will not recognize their father as father, their mother as mother, or their master as master. Conflicting emotions will completely poison their minds. No one will be able to lead them to do good."

"Well," said Ocean Dust, "it is then that I will manifest as a Buddha and teach."

The Buddha Quintessence of Jewels and all his sons admired the determination and courage of the young prince.

"Of all the flowers," they said, "you are like the most beautiful, the white lotus."

Then Ocean Dust made 500 great wishes to benefit all beings, which the other princes had not done.

There are many more stories relating how Shakyamuni Buddha engendered Bodhicitta in his past lives. These are among the most well-known.

4- Ceremony

There are several kinds of ceremonies for taking the Bodhisattva vow. Given here are the great lines of the ceremony in the tradition of Vast Action of Asanga. This ceremony has three parts: preparatory phase, body of the ceremony, and final phase.

Preparatory Phase
Request
The postulants make a request to the master who gives the Bodhisattva vow. In substance, they tell him or her, "In the same way that past Buddhas and Bodhisattvas at the beginning of the path have raised in themselves Bodhicitta—the wish to attain perfect Awakening—in the same way, I want to raise Bodhicitta in my mind now. Would you bestow the Bodhicitta vow upon me and allow me to take the promise of Awakening?"

Accumulation of Merit
The minor ordination (Sanskrit, *shramanera;* Tibetan, *getsul*) is taken in the presence of an abbot (Sanskrit, *upadhyaya;* Tibetan, *khenpo*). Major monastic

ordination is taken in the presence of the community of fully ordained monks (Sanskrit, *bhikshu;* Tibetan, *gelong*). As for the Bodhisattva vow, it is taken because of the accumulation of merit.

The accumulation of merit, culminating in the Bodhisattva vow, was accomplished in various ways by the great realized beings of the past. Some had offered great wealth; others who possessed nothing offered a handful of grass or a single flower; others offered only three prostrations.

For us, the best way to accumulate merit is certainly to use the *Seven-Branch Prayer*. To do so, we turn to all the Buddhas and Bodhisattvas and to the master who gives the vow. We then imagine that we produce an infinite number of bodies similar to our own to successively accomplish the seven branches:

1- We prostrate to pay homage to the Buddhas, Bodhisattvas, and the master.

2- We present them with offerings of all pleasant things in the universe, real, or created in our imagination.

3- We regret all negative acts done with body, speech, and mind since time without beginning.

4- We rejoice at all positive acts and beneficial activity accomplished by the Buddhas, Bodhisattvas, and ordinary beings.

5- We pray to the Buddhas and Bodhisattvas to turn the Wheel of the Dharma.

6- We plead for them to remain in this world for the benefit of all beings.

7- We dedicate the merit accumulated under the first six branches to the following intention, "By the merit of these six branches, may the precious Bodhicitta be born within my mind, and may I take the Bodhisattva vow."

Body of the Ceremony
Vow of Aspiring Bodhicitta

It has been said that everywhere there is space, there are beings; everywhere there are beings, there are conflicting emotions; everywhere there are conflicting emotions, negative karma is accumulated. From negative karma, the suffering of beings occurs.

It is said that all beings in samsara, without exception, were in our past lives, since time without beginning, our mother or our father. All these past mothers and fathers wandering in the ocean of cyclic existence for a long time are subjected to numberless sufferings. They have no one to protect or save them.

Reflecting on this situation, we form the sincere wish that all may become free of suffering and meet happiness. We engender love and compassion toward them.

This love and compassion, the foundation of Bodhicitta, must be impartial. In general, we have the tendency to classify beings into three categories: those we love and consider close to us; those who leave us indifferent and whom we place at a distance; and those whom we do not love and therefore reject, placing them even further away. True love, however, does not accept these categories. It does not embrace some beings to the detriment of others but takes into account all beings and their aspiration to have happiness and avoid suffering.

At present, we do not have the power to help the infinite number of beings, liberate them from suffering, and make them happy. We gain this power by thinking, "From now on, starting today, I commit myself to attain perfect Buddhahood—a state purified from all imperfections, endowed with all qualities, radiating love for all beings like a mother's love for her only child." Such is the essence of the vow of aspiring Bodhicitta.

To begin the ceremony, the postulants prostrate three times, place their right knee on the ground, join hands at the heart level, and repeat the words of the vow of aspiring Bodhicitta, after the master.

The meaning of this vow is:

"Buddhas and Bodhisattvas of the ten directions, and you also master, please turn your thoughts to me. Relying on the power of the merit acquired by the practice of giving, ethic, and other virtues, whether I have accomplished them myself or I have lead others to accomplish them; like the Buddhas and Bodhisattvas of the past have raised the wish to attain perfect and unsurpassable Awakening for the benefit of all beings, in the same way, beginning today and until I attain the heart of Awakening, I also commit myself to maintain the wish of attaining Awakening.

"When I attain Awakening, I will lead the beings dwelling in the three inferior realms to the three superior realms. I will lead those in the three superior realms who are subjected to conflicting emotions and karma to tranquility; I will encourage those who dwell in tranquility in order that they commit themselves to the Great Vehicle; I will establish the Bodhisattvas of the Great Vehicle in perfect Buddhahood."

This statement is repeated three times. During the third repetition, thinking of all beings, the postulants will say, "For the benefit of all beings, I will obtain perfect Awakening." They then promise from this instant on to attain this goal.

"... beginning today and until I attain the heart of Awakening, I also commit myself to maintain the wish of attaining Awakening. When I attain Awakening, I will lead the beings dwelling in the three inferior realms to the three superior realms. I will lead those in the three superior realms who are subjected to conflicting emotions and karma to tranquility; I will encourage those who dwell in tranquility in order that they commit themselves to the Great Vehicle; I will establish the Bodhisattvas of the Great Vehicle in perfect Buddhahood."

This promise is made in the presence of all Buddhas and Bodhisattvas of the ten directions. By repeating this statement, we eliminate distraction and imprint upon ourselves a personal commitment to reach the precise goal of helping all beings.

At the end of this third repetition, the master snaps his or her fingers and says, *"tap ynno,"* meaning that all those present have fully received the vow. They shall answer, *"lekso,"* (it is excellent) and make three prostrations again.

In this way, the vow of aspiring Bodhicitta is taken. In the tradition of the Profound View, vows of aspiring Bodhicitta and realizing Bodhicitta are taken simultaneously; while in the tradition of the Vast Action that we are following here, the vows are taken separately, at least in the extended versions of the ritual.

Vow of Realizing Bodhicitta
The postulants first recite a request to receive the vow of realizing Bodhicitta. Then, the master asks them questions in order to learn of any obstacles to taking the vow. The master in particular asks them:
- if they can follow the precepts and conduct of a Bodhisattva who acts to benefit all beings
- if, as beginners embarking on the path, they have no fear of committing errors regarding the precepts

of Bodhicitta; are they prepared to commit themselves

- whether they rejoice in the infinite benefits resulting from Bodhicitta

- if they have heard and understood the teachings on Bodhicitta, and if they have faith in them

- if they wish to work for the benefit of all beings

- if they take this vow without constraint

After the master has judged their aptitude to receive the vow, the postulants ask him or her to bestow the vow upon them.

Following this request, the master agrees to bestow the vow upon them.

While taking this vow, the postulant must keep in mind altruistic motivation. During the vow of aspiring Bodhicitta, we engage to attain perfect Buddhahood to free all beings from suffering and to bring them happiness. The commitment is to the *goal*, Buddhahood. The vow of realizing Bodhicitta, on the other hand, is directed to the *means* necessary to attain this goal: the observance of the Bodhicitta precepts, the practice of the six paramitas, the elimination of mistakes, and the respect of the three ethics (ethic that avoids negative acts, ethic that practices positive acts, and ethic accomplishing benefit for others). All the Buddhas of the past have trained in this way; it is also the way of the present Buddha, and it will be the way of future Buddhas. The vow of realizing Bodhicitta, therefore, consists of promising to follow this path, accomplishing all that must be accomplished, and avoiding all that must be avoided.

The master asks the postulants three times if they wish to follow this way, if they respect this path, and if they make the commitment to follow this path. They answer that they wish to do so, and that they make the commitment to do so.

The third answer seals the promise. The disciples have then fully received the vow of realizing Bodhicitta. This completes the vow of the Bodhisattva.

Conclusion
Addressing the Buddhas and Bodhisattvas
The master stands up, makes a prostration in each of the ten directions (the four cardinal points, the four intermediary directions, the zenith, and the nadir) to the Buddhas who dwell there, and offers them flowers by tossing the blossoms skyward.

Addressing the Buddhas, the master lets them know that on this day, in his or her presence these disciples have taken the Bodhisattva vow and are now members of the Bodhisattva family.

Buddhas and Bodhisattvas' Joy
Given that the Bodhisattva vow is an extremely beneficial act with extensive benefits, the Buddhas and Bodhisattvas from all the pure lands are informed that this vow has been taken on this very day, and they profoundly rejoice. From this day forward, through the sight conferred by their omniscience, they will consider us always as their beloved sons and daughters.

Talking about the Vow with Mindfulness
For the disciple, receiving the Bodhisattva vow implies some preliminary qualities such as belonging to the Mahayana family, that is, having a natural inclination for love and compassion, and also having had the good fortune to be taught by a master the necessity and benefits of the vow and having understood its importance. We can only talk about the vow mindfully. It is preferable not to try to convince people who have not had the necessary preparation of its greatness, or people who, because of their mentality cannot understand it. In our residual age, such people would be at risk; instead of being interested, they would be scared and adopt an attitude of rejection that would harm them.

Explanation of the Precepts

The master reveals the different precepts relating to the vow of aspiring Bodhicitta and to the vow of realizing Bodhicitta. These precepts are numerous and various (they are explained in detail in section two of this book). The main precepts, those that we must especially respect, are as follows:

A- Precepts of Aspiring Bodhicitta

1- NOT TO REJECT ANY BEING FROM OUR MIND

What does it mean? If someone does something to displease us, and we consider this person an enemy, or if moved by anger, we entertain a resentful attitude leading us to thinking, from now on, we will do nothing for this person; and that we will never aid him or her when the opportunity arises, then we reject this person from our mind. We must guard against this attitude because we have taken the commitment to attain Awakening, to help *all* beings, without exception. We cannot make any exceptions, even for one person. Anger can momentarily lead us to nourish such a thought. We reject others from our mind and break our vow only if:
- without restraining ourselves, we persist for a long time in this attitude
- we feel no regret
- we are happy with this attitude

- we consider this attitude justified and a positive quality

2- REMINDING OURSELVES OF THE BENEFITS OF BODHICITTA

By the simple fact that Bodhicitta has been imprinted on our mind, we are purified from many past negative acts and we accumulate much merit. We are, from this time, on the path of the Great Vehicle. Therefore, we must often remind ourselves of the extremely great benefits of Bodhicitta.

3- PROCEEDING TO THE ACCUMULATION OF MERIT AND WISDOM to let Bodhicitta develop within us.

4- RENEWING THE VOW EACH DAY

If possible, we should renew the vow six times in a 24-hour period (three times during the day and three times at night) or, at least three times during the day (in the morning when we get up, at noon, and in the evening before going to bed) by simply reciting Atisha's four lines which include taking refuge and taking the Bodhisattva vow.

In the Buddha, Dharma, and great Sangha
I take refuge until Awakening
Through my practice of giving and other perfections
May I attain Buddhahood for the benefit of beings.

In our mind, we recite these four lines in front of the Buddhas and remember their meaning.

5- AVOIDING THE FOUR BLACK ACTS AND PRACTICING THE FOUR WHITE ACTS

The four black acts are:
- intentionally misleading our master or parents through self-interest
- regretting having accomplished positive acts, that others accomplished them, or to cause those who have accomplished positive acts to regret them
- criticizing saints
- having a dishonest attitude toward others

The four white acts are opposite to the four black acts:
- being sincere toward our master and parents
- rejoicing in positive acts accomplished by ourselves or others
- praising saints
- being honest with others

These five points are the main precepts of aspiring Bodhicitta. There exist many other precepts which are classified in various ways by the two traditions of the Bodhisattva vow. The Profound View lineage presents 14 root transgressions (that can be reduced to five or one) that we must avoid and 80 secondary transgressions; the Vast Action lineage has four root transgressions and 46 secondary transgressions.

These various presentations are not contradictory but correspond to several points of view. Some people are distressed when they see long lists of precepts. They are afraid of observing so many rules and believe that it is beyond their ability. Still, others like precision and need very clearly marked limits. They appreciate lists that answer each situation in detail. The Buddhas and Bodhisattvas, wishing to impart a teaching adapted to one's capabilities and way of understanding, proposed various approaches that are short or detailed, simple or complex.

What is the most important precept to respect when we take the Bodhisattva vow? It is to never be separated from an attitude of love and compassion and the will to benefit others without ever rejecting a single being from our mind. If, on this basis, we bring aid and support those who need them as much as possible, we maintain the essence of the precepts of Bodhicitta.

B- Precepts of Realizing Bodhicitta
To engage in following the precepts of realizing Bodhicitta consists of practicing the six paramitas:
- giving
- ethic
- patience
- diligence
- concentration
- wisdom

Rejoicing
We rejoice in taking the Bodhisattva vow and consequently entering the family of the Conquerors (Bodhisattvas). From that day forward, our human existence is meaningful. Measuring our good fortune, we feel joy and happiness.

Dedication
We make wishes to be able to maintain the practice of Bodhicitta until we attain Awakening and to accomplish an extremely vast activity for the benefit of others similar to the activity of Avalokiteshvara and other great Bodhisattvas.

སངས་རྒྱས་ཆོས་དང་ཚོགས་ཀྱི་མཆོག་རྣམས་ལ།

།བྱང་ཆུབ་བར་དུ་བདག་ནི་སྐྱབས་སུ་མཆི།

།བདག་གིས་སྦྱིན་སོགས་བགྱིས་པའི་བསོད་ནམས་ཀྱིས།

།འགྲོ་ལ་ཕན་ཕྱིར་སངས་རྒྱས་འགྲུབ་པར་ཤོག །

SANGYE CHO TANG TSO GY CHO NAM LA

JANGCHUB BARTU DANI KYAB SU CHI

DA GYI JIN SO GYPEI SONAM GI

DROLA PEN CHIR SANGYE DRUP PAR SHO

In the Buddha, Dharma, and great Community
I take refuge until Awakening
Through practicing giving and other perfections
May I attain Buddhahood
for the benefit of beings.

This verse of four lines was composed by the great Indian Buddhist master Atisha, who spent many years in Tibet in the 11th century.

Reciting it at least three times a day (morning, noon, and evening), we maintain the Bodhisattva vow by renewing it.

The two first lines, "In the Buddha, Dharma, and great community, I take refuge until Awakening," are an expression of taking refuge; the great community designates the gathering of those who have at least attained the first stage of a Bodhisattva.

The third line, "Through practicing giving and other perfections," states the vow of realizing Bodhicitta; "giving and other perfections," refers to the six paramitas.

The fourth verse, "May I attain Buddhahood for the benefit of beings," states the vow of aspiring Bodhicitta.

Asanga (4th century C.E.) founder of the Yogachara school; he received many teachings from Maitreya Buddha of whom he had a vision.
It is from Maitreya that Asanga obtained the transmission of the lineage of the Bodhisattva vow called "Vast Understanding" which he initiated.

PART TWO: PRECEPTS

We pray the Bodhisattva "Quintessence of the sky"
(Sanskrit, Akashagarbha; Tibetan, Namkhai Nyingpo)
when we want to purify ourselves of a transgression.

1- *Precepts of Aspiring Bodhicitta*

By taking the Bodhisattva vow, we commit to attain Awakening for the benefit of all beings. Transgressions of the vow are actions or attitudes that pull us farther away from our goal, slowing its accomplishment or acting contrary to the benefit of beings. It is why the Bodhisattva ethic request that we avoid them.

The precepts of aspiring Bodhicitta mainly consist of keeping us from what is called the root or secondary transgressions.

The two transmission lineages of the Bodhisattva vow present slightly different versions of these transgressions. There are several lists of these precepts. Here, we follow those given by Jamgon Lodro Taye in his *Treasury of Knowledge (Sheja Zo)*. According to this text, the Profound View tradition presents a list of root transgressions whose number varies (14,5, or 1) and 80 secondary transgressions (which will not be enumerated here), whereas the list from the Vast Action tradition comprises four root transgressions and 46 secondary transgressions.

We will here consider successively:
- the root transgressions according to the tradition of the Profound View
- the root transgressions according to the tradition of the Vast Action
- the secondary transgressions according to the tradition of the Vast Action
- the transgressions common to both traditions
- how to purify ourselves from these transgressions

Root Transgressions according to the Tradition of the Profound View
Nagarjuna's tradition of the Profound View gives three different lists of root transgressions, referring to individuals of superior, mediocre, or lesser capabilities.

THE FOURTEEN ROOT TRANSGRESSIONS OF INDIVIDUALS OF SUPERIOR CAPABILITIES ARE DIVIDED INTO THREE GROUPS
- the five king transgressions (1-5)
- the five minister transgressions (reduced to number 6)
- the eight people transgressions (7-14)
   The complete list comprises 18 points. However, since the four transgressions of the ministers are similar to the four transgressions of the king, it is usually reduced from 18 to 14 points which follow.

The king, the minister, and the people correspond to the social strata that existed in ancient India. The formulation of some transgressions, therefore, may have no application in most contemporary societies.

The Five King Transgressions

1- STEALING THE THREE JEWELS. Taking goods consecrated to the Three Jewels (statues, sacred texts, temples, and stupas) or goods that have been offered to the monks' community.

2- ABANDONING THE DHARMA, whether it is the Great Vehicle or Small Vehicle; particularly in the case of a monarch who orders abandoning the Dharma, whether in its totality or by condemning one vehicle to profit another.

3- HARMING MONASTICS, whether the monastics are respecting their vows or have broken their vows, by condemning, whipping, or imprisoning them.

4- ACCOMPLISHING ANY ONE OF THE FIVE ACTS WITH IMMEDIATE CONSEQUENCES:

killing one's father; killing one's mother; killing an arhat; creating a schism in the Sangha; making a Buddha bleed with the intention of harming. These five acts are in the category of the transgressions particular to the king abusing his power and giving into the temptation of accomplishing them. Although the risk to accomplish these acts is higher for a king than for other persons, the same acts accomplished by an ordinary being would also be a serious transgression of Bodhisattva ethic.

5- PROFESSING NIHILISTIC OPINIONS: officially professing that the law of karma does not exist, that there are no past or future lives, and so on. Nihilistic opinions lead to negative activity.

The Five Minister Transgressions
(The first four transgressions are similar to those of a king and, therefore, are not counted again in this list)

6- DESTROYING A CITY: a city is designated here as a human group, whatever its size. The minister is equivalent to a prime minister, the person to whom the king delegates power, and who can give the order to eliminate a city or destroy a people in a war situation.

The Eight People Transgressions
These eight transgressions concern anyone who has taken the Bodhisattva vow and, unlike kings and ministers, does not have any specific power. Most of these transgressions concern us more directly.

7- TEACHING EMPTINESS TO A PERSON NOT READY FOR IT. A person who gives teachings on the profound meaning of emptiness to someone whose mind is not ready to receive them, will risk shaking the recipient's confidence and scare him or her.

8- DIVERTING THE PERSON WHO HAS TAKEN THE BODHISATTVA VOW FROM AWAKENING; discouraging this person engaged in the Great Vehicle (which alone can lead to complete Buddhahood) by saying that he or she cannot not practice the six paramitas and that it would be better for him or her to turn to the Small Vehicle.

9- MAKING SOMEONE ABANDON THE SMALL VEHICLE; advising the person who has a natural affinity for the Small Vehicle to abandon it to enter the Great Vehicle.

10- BELIEVING THAT THE SMALL VEHICLE DOES NOT NEUTRALIZE CONFLICTING EMOTIONS and making others believe that, in other words, professing that the Small Vehicle is without efficiency and is useless.

11- PRAISING ONESELF AND CRITICIZING OTHERS. To profit from or to advertise one's good reputation; praising oneself (declaring that one has understood and realized everything) whereas one does not deserve it, and criticizing others when they do not deserve it.

12- BEING PROUD OF ONE'S REALIZATION. Although it is untrue, being proud to be versed in profound practices, pretending to have attained realization, and doing this with a goal of obtaining profit or fame.

13- DIVERTING OFFERINGS MADE TO A MONASTERY by using corrupt means and calumny when one is in a position of power, or accepting money or goods coming from this.

14- ABANDONING THE SUPPORT OF A PRACTITIONER TO GIVE TO A STUDENT. A long time ago in India, as well as in Tibet, practitioners retired in solitude and lived on the food given to them. This food, their only means of subsistence, was essential to pursue their meditations. Ceasing to give food to practitioners (or advising others to do so) or preferring to give it, for instance, to those who are happy with only studying, would create a great obstacle for the practitioners.

THE FOUR ROOT TRANSGRESSIONS OF INDIVIDUALS WITH MEDIOCRE CAPABILITIES

1- COMPLETELY REJECTING BODHICITTA.

2- NOT GIVING TO THOSE WHO ASK because of attachment or stinginess, whether it is for material goods or the Dharma.

3- HITTING SOMEONE IN ANGER.

4- TEACHING FALSE DHARMA. Giving a teaching with a spiritual appearance but which is only an invention created by conflicting emotions.

THE UNIQUE ROOT PRECEPT OF INDIVIDUALS OF INFERIOR CAPABILITIES

KEEPING ASPIRING BODHICITTA is the only precept that individuals of lesser capabilities must observe. It is the precept that epitomizes all others. Keeping aspiring Bodhicitta simply means that from the perspective of Awakening, we should keep an attitude of love and compassion, a well-wishing feeling rejecting no one. In other words, we should not look for self-liberation, but for Awakening for the benefit of beings.

Root Transgressions according to the Tradition of Vast Action

Asanga's tradition of Vast Action gathers the root transgressions into four points.

1- PRAISING ONESELF AND CRITICIZING OTHERS with the intention of receiving offerings, of acting like someone important, or of gaining profit.

2- NOT GIVING MATERIAL GOODS OR THE DHARMA, because of stinginess, to those who are needy, the poor, or those who request the teaching.

3- NOT ACCEPTING APOLOGIES from a person who has harmed us or offended us in one way or another, but punishing this person.

4- REJECTING MAHAYANA. Criticizing and dismissing the Mahayana teachings and propagating a false dharma.

Secondary Transgressions according to the Tradition of Vast Action

The tradition of Vast Action adds a list of 46 secondary transgressions to the four root transgressions. According to the *Treasury of Knowledge*, they are organized in the following way:

• 34 acts contrary to the development of spiritual qualities (1-34)

- 7 acts contrary to giving (1-7)
- 9 acts contrary to ethic (8-16)
- 4 acts contrary to patience (17-20)
- 3 acts contrary to diligence (21-23)
- 3 acts contrary to concentration (24-26)
- 8 acts contrary to knowledge (27-34)

• 12 acts contrary to the accomplishment of benefiting others (35-46)

The detailed list of these 46 transgressions is as follows:

1- MAKING NO OFFERING TO THE THREE JEWELS

2- FOLLOWING ONE'S OWN DESIRE

3- NOT ACCORDING RESPECT TO ELDERS

4- NOT ANSWERING QUESTIONS WHEN ONE IS ASKED

5- NOT ANSWERING AN INVITATION

6- VIOLENTLY REFUSING A GIFT because of pride or contempt

7- NOT EXPLAINING THE DHARMA TO WHOMEVER WISHES TO RECEIVE IT

8- REJECTING A PERSON WHO HAS DAMAGED HIS OR HER VOWS

9- NOT STUDYING THE DHARMA and not observing the rules of ethic when it is necessary to strengthen the confidence of others

10- HAVING ONLY LITTLE ENERGY TO BENEFIT BEINGS

11- NOT PERFORMING AN APPARENTLY NEGATIVE ACT although this act must be done out of compassion

12- VOLUNTARILY EARNING A LIVELIHOOD BY DISHONEST MEANS. There are five dishonest ways to make a living (flattery, extortion of money, constraint, deceit, and corruption). We can neither use these means for ourselves nor accept offerings gained by these means.

13- TAKING PLEASURE IN MEANINGLESS ACTIVITIES. Devoting much time to activities that are only diversions (sports, shows, games, drinking, useless conversations, and so on) when this time could be profitably spent in the practice of the Dharma.

14- WISHING TO BE RELEASED FROM SAMSARA ALONE, under the influence of attachment.

15- NOT AVOIDING HAVING A BAD REPUTATION.

16- NOT PUTTING AWAY CONFLICTING EMOTIONS.

17- RESPONDING TO OFFENSES. When someone hits, insults us, and so on, answering the offense by offending; meeting anger with anger; blows with blows; criticism with criticism.

18- REJECTING THOSE WHO FEEL RESENTFUL TOWARD US rather than trying to make peace.

19- NOT ACCEPTING APOLOGIES FROM OTHERS.

20- GETTING ANGRY.

21- SEARCHING FOR DISCIPLES TO GAIN PROFIT OR RESPECT.

22- NOT LOOKING FOR WAYS TO ELIMINATE LAZINESS, procrastination, nonchalance, and all that makes us waste time.

23- ENGAGING IN USELESS CONVERSATION about the world's problems.

24- NOT PRACTICING MEDITATION and not seeking necessary instructions.

25- NOT ELIMINATING OBSTACLES TO MEDITATION such as distraction, sleepiness, or doubt.

26- GETTING ATTACHED TO THE PLEASANT EXPERIENCES PRODUCED BY MEDITATION.

27- HAVING DISRESPECT FOR THE HINAYANA.

28- DISCARDING MAHAYANA TO DEVOTE ONESELF MORE TO HINAYANA. When one is engaged on the Mahayana path, returning to Hinayana.

29- NEGLECTING THE STUDY OF THE DHARMA TO STUDY TEMPORAL SUBJECTS.

30- WHEN DEVOTING ONESELF TO THE MAHAYANA, FINDING PLEASURE IN HINAYANA AND SECULAR SUBJECTS.

31- NOT BEING INTERESTED IN THE TEACHINGS OF THE MAHAYANA.

32- NOT SEEKING THE DHARMA because of pride or laziness, not listening to the teachings, or not reading books to better understand the Dharma.

33- PRAISING ONESELF AND CRITICIZING OTHERS.

34- NOT TRUSTING THE MEANING BUT TRUSTING THE WORDS; especially trusting our own understanding of a text rather than the meaning explained by a master.

35- NOT OFFERING HELP to those who really need it.

36- NOT TAKING CARE OF SICK PEOPLE.

37- NOT SEEKING WAYS TO SOOTHE SUFFERING, pain, and sorrow.

38- NOT WARNING CARELESS PEOPLE, not taking care of disciples, or caring for those under our responsibility.

39- BEING UNGRATEFUL TOWARD THOSE WHO HAVE HELPED US.

40- NOT RELIEVING THE SUFFERING OF OTHERS, whether this suffering is material or mental.

41- NOT GIVING TO THOSE WHO WISH TO HAVE RICHNESS although we can do so.

42- NOT HELPING PEOPLE AROUND US.

43- NOT ACTING ACCORDING TO THE MENTALITY OF OTHERS.

44- NOT PRAISING THE QUALITIES OF OTHER PEOPLE.

45- NOT STOPPING THE MISDEEDS OF HARMFUL BEINGS.

46- NOT USING MIRACLES OR SUPRA KNOWLEDGE when it is necessary to guide others.

Precepts Common to Both Traditions

The following transgressions are common to the two traditions.

1- REJECTING ANY BEING FROM OUR MIND

2- ENGAGING IN THE FOUR BLACK ACTS, which are:
- deceiving our master or parents
- regretting positive actions
- criticizing realized beings
- harboring a dishonest attitude

3- NOT ENGAGING IN THE FOUR WHITE ACTS, which are:
- being sincere with our master and parents
- rejoicing in positive actions
- praising realized beings
- being honest with others

Avoiding the totality of these transgressions constitutes the precepts belonging to the aspiring Bodhicitta. The precepts of realizing Bodhicitta, for both traditions, are the six paramitas.

Purifying Ourselves of Transgressions
FOUR DETERMINING FACTORS

When we commit one of the transgressions, we go against our vow. However, the transgression is only completed when four determining factors are present.
- continuing to engage in the transgression
- feeling no regret, no shame, no embarrassment

- being satisfied to have acted like this
- considering the accomplished act as a quality instead of a defect

If not all of these four factors are present, it does not mean that there is no fault, but only that the fault is less serious. The fault is considered only of medium severity when two or three factors are present, and minor when only one factor is present.

In any case, it is necessary to purify oneself.

PURIFYING OURSELVES OF ILL-WISHING

Given that by taking the Bodhisattva vow, we engage ourselves to help all beings and continually keep a kind attitude toward them, we might wonder whether a simple thought of ill-will, which can still occur in our mind, will break the vow. A simple thought of ill-will does not break the Bodhisattva vow; it slightly damages it.

However, when thoughts of going against the Bodhisattva vow occur in our mind—if for example, we think that a certain person is a blameworthy person and that we will never do anything to help this person—we must purify ourselves. This purification can be done in a simple way. We become aware of the erroneous tendency of the thought, we regret it, and reaffirm our Bodhisattva commitment: "To accomplish the benefit of all beings, I commit myself to attain Buddhahood, I will help and relieve the suffering of all beings." To give strength to this commitment and fully counter the initial negative thought, we remind ourselves that this person—like all beings—has been our mother, father, or friend in past lives, and then has brought to us all that can be brought by a mother, father, or friend. We also remind ourselves of the immense positive qualities of love and compassion as opposed to the difficulties and suffering that result from aggressiveness and ill-will.

PURIFYING OURSELVES OF BREAKING THE VOW

Although all the transgressions go against the Bodhisattva vow, completely breaking the vow is mentally abandoning one or several beings and deciding to do nothing for their benefit.

As we have seen earlier, however, the vow is fully broken only if this abandonment is accompanied by the four determining factors and nothing is done to change our attitude over a long period of time—one year for example. We must then take the vow again completely, during a formal ceremony in the presence of a lama.

If only three of the four factors are present, it is sufficient to repent before two people having taken the Bodhisattva vow; for one factor, in the presence of only one person having taken the vow.

PURIFYING OURSELVES OF A TRANSGRESSION

Purifying a transgression is done individually. Dawn is the best time to perform it. We turn to the east and invoke the Bodhisattva called "Quintessence of the sky" (Sanskrit, Akashagarbha; Tibetan, Namkhai Nyingpo) to pray to him.

It is said in the sutras that the Bodhisattva Quintessence of the Sky, by the power of the specific wishes he has formulated for the benefit of those who break the Bodhisattva vow, appears at dawn so they can purify themselves. It is why it is good to turn to him to unveil all that contradicts the Bodhisattva ethic and repent.

The best method of confession is to recite the *Sutra of the Three Heaps* also called the *Confession to the Thirty-five Buddhas* divided in three sections: heap of homages, heap of confessions, and heap of dedications.

In connection with the Vajrayana, we can use the Vajrasattva practice and recitation of the mantra in which all forms of purification are collected.

Shantideva who lived from 650 to 750 was a great poet and a realized being. His major work, the Bodhisattvacharyavatara describes the commitments and the path of a bodhisattva.

2- Overview on the Six Paramitas

The practice of the Dharma first teaches us to avoid anything that could harm others by our conduct, speech, and thoughts. However, we should not pause at this stage. We need to go further and adopt an attitude beneficial to others. In the Great Vehicle, this conduct is expressed by the six paramitas, the six transcendent perfections. These six paramitas form the path of the Bodhisattva to attain Awakening that the Bodhisattva wants to attain for the benefit of all beings. Therefore, the paramitas are *the precepts of realizing Bodhicitta*. They are:
- giving
- ethic
- patience
- diligence
- concentration
- wisdom

Their order is not accidental. They are gradually classified from the easiest to the most difficult or from the most obvious to the more subtle.

Each of these paramitas is divided into three aspects.

1- Giving
Giving Material Goods
Giving is accompanied by a thought of compassion and is directed toward those who need material goods—food, clothes, and all that may be necessary.

Providing Security
We may help those whose lives are in danger, those who are touched by sickness, those who are punished, or those threatened by wild animals. When we protect those who are in fear and in danger, we practice giving different forms of security.

Giving the Dharma
The two first types of giving apply to physical aid. Giving the Dharma aids the mind. It is giving the Buddha's teaching, whether one explains it directly or helps create the conditions for its development.

2- Ethic
Ethic That Maintains Vows
Ethic consists of avoiding negative activity in our bodily conduct, speech, or thoughts. In particular, it is restraining from any harmful act done to

others, whether this is generally or more precisely related to the monastics or lay practitioners vows.

Ethic That Accomplishes Accumulations
This second type of ethic is not restricted to avoiding negative activity but works for positive effects such as accomplishing positive acts, and accumulation of merit and wisdom.

Ethic That Accomplishes Benefits for Others
The first two kinds of ethic, although founded on our relationship with others, are done first of all for our own benefit: protecting us from suffering resulting from negative activity and searching for benefits stemming from positive activity for ourselves. The third type of ethic has another perspective and concerns only benefiting others.

3- Patience
Patience in the Face of Enemies
People can harm us in various ways by attacking us physically, using harmful words against us; and by having ill thoughts toward us. These people are then seen as our "enemies," whether temporarily or for the long term. The first kind of patience is patience toward these enemies.

There are various methods to use in applying patience.

First, we can remind ourselves that on a karmic level, if someone creates some difficulties, it is because we have created difficulties for this person in a past life. We are, therefore, repaid for our own acts.

We can also reflect that in reality, the person who hurts us is only an appearance of an illusory nature, similar to what occurs in a dream. Although there appears to be an enemy, an aggression committed by this enemy, and a victim of this enemy (that is ourselves), in truth, the threefold elements of the situation lack reality in themselves and are only illusory projections of the mind.

A third method is to discover the real object of our anger or resentment. When someone attacks us, we are angry with the person perceived as a human body in its totality, endowed with forms and colors. However, on reflection, what is truly harming us? Let us suppose that someone wounds us with a knife. What hurts us is really the knife. However, we do not get angry at the knife because we know that it is only inert matter, with no freedom of action. In fact, it is the hand of the person who directed the knife. But we do not become angry at the hand because it is not the hand that decides to act. The object of our anger is therefore the aggressor that is the physical person. However, this physical person is not responsible. He or she only obeys the mind. As for the mind of the aggressor, can we say that it acts freely? No, we cannot, because it is under the influence of conflicting emotions such as hatred or anger. From then on, our reaction to our aggressor must not be to become angry but rather to engender a feeling of compassion born of the understanding of the state of slavery in which the mind of our enemy is held. Far from enjoying freedom, his or her mind is subject to the conflicting emotions, which it obeys like a prisoner obeys a guardian. If we were to experience anger as a response, it should not be directed against our aggressor—who is a victim of enslavement—but against that which enslaves his or her mind, the conflicting emotions which must be suppressed. It is only because we lack this understanding that we abandon patience for unjustified anger.

Patience in the Face of Suffering
Our tendency is to give importance to suffering even if it is small. We absolutely want to avoid it, to get rid of it. Because of this attitude, a little suffering becomes a big problem. Conversely, if we know how to bear suffering, if we stay steady inside, even great suffering becomes small suffering. The less patient we are with suffering, the greater

effect it has. The more patient we are with suffering, the more it loses its power over us.

More particularly, when we begin the practice of Dharma, it is possible that we will meet with some difficulties or things that are not convenient for us. Perhaps, we think that we will never be able to practice correctly, that it is too difficult physically, mentally, and so on. If we allow ourselves to sink into this attitude, we will become discouraged and lazy. The least difficulty will become a serious obstacle. On the contrary, we must know how to persevere, whatever the difficulties, and apply ourselves to the Dharma with courage and continuity of practice. We then will be able to study and meditate in a fruitful way.

Patience in the Face of Dharma Truths
Many truths are difficult to understand, even to accept, such as the notion of past and future lives, the law of karma, the functioning of samsara, its illusory nature, the extraordinary qualities of the Buddhas and Bodhisattvas, and so on. We cannot see for ourselves or verify the truth of such notions. Our mind has the opportunity neither to test them nor to embrace them. It is why we are easily filled with doubt. There is also the need for the patience that permits us to accept what we cannot fully understand. It is true that it is impossible for us to

see the subtleties of the law of karma, but we accept them. It is true that qualities of the Buddhas and Bodhisattvas exceed our understanding, but we accept that possibility.

4-Diligence
Armor of Diligence
A resolute attitude, the determination to practice the Dharma and attain Awakening, and the assurance to do it are the first kind of diligence. It is called the armor of diligence. According to Gampopa, wearing this armor is thinking, "From now on until all beings are established in perfect Awakening, I will never abandon diligence in the practice of virtue."

Applied Diligence
The second kind of diligence concerns practice itself. It consists of persevering in all circumstances, even when we encounter obstacles, without giving way to discouragement or laziness.

Insatiable Diligence
The practice progressively leads to various results and levels. Insatiable diligence consists of never being satisfied with obtained results, nor ever being willing to pause before full Awakening is attained. It consists of never thinking, "I have accomplished

enough virtuous acts, I have done enough practices. I can now stop."

5- Concentration
First Step of Concentration
The first step of concentration is to be reached through the meditation of mental calming (Sanskrit, shamata; Tibetan, shinay) a state where body and mind experience great peace and ease.

Second Step of Concentration
It consists of developing qualities inherent in the meditation in addition to the peace and happiness felt during the meditation.

Third Step of Concentration
The third step leads to the development of meditative states that permit us to accomplish others' benefit.

6- Wisdom
Temporal Wisdom
Temporal wisdom applies to the various areas of studies concerned only with the present world, such as the fields of science or culture. This wisdom is qualified as obscured because of its limitations.

Inferior Spiritual Wisdom

Inferior spiritual wisdom proceeds from the study and practice of the Small Vehicle. It is inferior because it realizes only the lack of existence by itself of the individual, of the "me," the root of samsaric existence.

Superior Spiritual Wisdom

Issued from the Great Vehicle, superior spiritual wisdom adds to the realization of the lack of existence in and by itself of all phenomena the realization of the lack of existence by itself of the individual.

The Sutra of the Three Heaps

The Sutra of the Three Heaps (Sanskrit, *Triskandharma Sutra;* Tibetan, *P'ungpo sum pai do*), also called *Bodhisattvas' Repentance of Transgressions*, or *Repentance in front of the 35 Buddhas,* is a practice that purifies the transgressions of vows in general and the transgression of the Bodhisattva vow in particular.

Its origin is as follows. A group of 35 monks, having taken the Bodhisattva vow, inadvertently provoked the death of a child when they were begging. Wishing to purify themselves, they asked Upali, one of the closest disciples of the Buddha, to request from his master a method of appropriate repentance. The Buddha uttered a brief sutra, in which the 35 Buddhas are mentioned relating to the 35 monks. It is said that at the moment Shakyamuni Buddha uttered this sutra, his body radiated a powerful light within which 34 Buddhas appeared and circled him in space. (Shakyamuni Buddha is counted as one of the 35 Buddhas.) The 35 monks prostrated, made offerings, awakened Bodhicitta within their minds, and took refuge in the Buddhas. They repented their faults, and by this very fact, attained the Bodhisattvas stages.

The recitation of this sutra is quite common among Tibetans. Tsongkhapa, the founder of the Gelugpa school, is famous for having made 100,000 prostrations in front of each of the 35 Buddhas.

The three heaps contained in the sutra are:
- heap of homages
- heap of repentances
- heap of dedications

༄༅། །སེམས་ཅན་ཐམས་ཅད་རྟག་པར་བླ་མ་ལ་སྐྱབས་སུ་མཆིའོ། །སངས་རྒྱས་ལ་སྐྱབས་སུ་མཆིའོ། །ཆོས་ལ་སྐྱབས་སུ་མཆིའོ། །དགེ་འདུན་ལ་སྐྱབས་སུ་མཆིའོ། །བཅོམ་ལྡན་འདས་དེ་བཞིན་གཤེགས་པ་དགྲ་བཅོམ་པ་ཡང་དག་པར་རྫོགས་པའི་སངས་རྒྱས་ཤཱཀྱ་ཐུབ་པ་ལ་ཕྱག་འཚལ་ལོ། །རྡོ་རྗེ་སྙིང་པོས་རབ་ཏུ་འཇོམས་པ་ལ་ཕྱག་འཚལ་ལོ། །རིན་ཆེན་འོད་འཕྲོ་ལ་ཕྱག་འཚལ་ལོ། །ཀླུ་དབང་གི་རྒྱལ་པོ་ལ་ཕྱག་འཚལ་ལོ། །དཔའ་བོའི་སྡེ་ལ་ཕྱག་འཚལ་ལོ། །དཔལ་དགྱེས་ལ་ཕྱག་འཚལ་ལོ། །རིན་ཆེན་མེ་ལ་ཕྱག་འཚལ་ལོ། །རིན་ཆེན་ཟླ་འོད་ལ་ཕྱག་འཚལ་ལོ། །མཐོང་བ་དོན་ཡོད་ལ་ཕྱག་འཚལ་ལོ། །རིན་ཆེན་ཟླ་བ་ལ་ཕྱག་འཚལ་ལོ། །དྲི་མ་མེད་པ་ལ་ཕྱག་འཚལ་ལོ། །དཔལ་བྱིན་ལ་ཕྱག་འཚལ་ལོ། །ཚངས་པ་ལ་ཕྱག་འཚལ་ལོ། །ཚངས་པས་བྱིན་ལ་ཕྱག་འཚལ་ལོ། །ཆུ་ལྷ་ལ་ཕྱག་འཚལ་ལོ། །ཆུ་ལྷའི་ལྷ་ལ་ཕྱག་འཚལ་ལོ། །དཔལ་བཟང་ལ་ཕྱག་འཚལ་ལོ། །ཙན་དན་དཔལ་ལ་ཕྱག་འཚལ་ལོ། །གཟི་བརྗིད་མཐའ་ཡས་ལ་ཕྱག་འཚལ་ལོ། །འོད་དཔལ་ལ་ཕྱག་འཚལ་ལོ། །མྱ་ངན་མེད་པའི་དཔལ་ལ་ཕྱག་འཚལ

94

The Sutra of the Three Heaps
For ever, I and all beings take refuge in the guru
We take refuge in the Buddha,
We take refuge in the Dharma,
We take refuge in the Sangha.

To Shakyamuni, the Perfect Buddha, the Conqueror, the Holder, the Transcendent One, the Thus-Gone, the One Victorious over the enemy, I pay homage. To the One who has fully conquered with the diamond essence, I pay homage.
To the *Jewel Radiating Light*, I pay homage.
To the *Sovereign King of Nagas*, I pay homage.
To the *Leader of Heroes*, I pay homage.
To the *Glorious Joy*, I pay homage.
To the *Jewel Fire*, I pay homage.
To the *Jewel Moonlight*, I pay homage.
To the *Meaningful Vision*, I pay homage.
To the *Jewel Moon*, I pay homage.
To the *Stainless One*, I pay homage.
To the *Glorious Giving*, I pay homage.
To the *Pure One*, I pay homage.
To the *Giving of Purity*, I pay homage.
To the *Water Deity*, I pay homage.
To the *God of Water Deities*, I pay homage.
To the *Glorious Goodness*, I pay homage.
To the *Glorious Sandalwood*, I pay homage.

ལོ། །སྲིད་མེད་ཀྱི་བུ་ལ་ཕྱག་འཚལ་ལོ། །མི་ཏྲ་ག་དཔལ་ལ་ཕྱག་འཚལ་
ལོ། །དེ་བཞིན་ག་ཤེགས་པ་ཚངས་པའི་འོད་ཟེར་རྣམ་པར་རོལ་པ་མངོན་
པར་མཐུན་པ་ལ་ཕྱག་འཚལ་ལོ། །དེ་བཞིན་ག་ཤེགས་པ་པདྨའི་འོད་ཟེར་
རྣམ་པར་རོལ་པ་མངོན་པར་མཐུན་པ་ལ་ཕྱག་འཚལ་ལོ། །ཕྱིར་དཔལ་ལ་
ཕྱག་འཚལ་ལོ། །དྲན་པའི་དཔལ་ལ་ཕྱག་འཚལ་ལོ། །མཚན་དཔལ་ཤིན་
ཏུ་ཡོངས་གྲགས་ལ་ཕྱག་འཚལ་ལོ། །དབང་པོའི་ཏོག་གི་རྒྱལ་མཚན་གྱི་
རྒྱལ་པོ་ལ་ཕྱག་འཚལ་ལོ། །ཤིན་ཏུ་རྣམ་པར་གནོན་པའི་དཔལ་ལ་ཕྱག་
འཚལ་ལོ། །གཡུལ་ལས་ཤིན་ཏུ་རྣམ་པར་རྒྱལ་བ་ལ་ཕྱག་འཚལ་ལོ།
།རྣམ་པར་གནོན་པས་ག་ཤེགས་པ་ལ་ཕྱག་འཚལ་ལོ། །ཀུན་ནས་སྣང་བ་
བཀོད་པའི་དཔལ་ལ་ཕྱག་འཚལ་ལོ། །རིན་ཆེན་པདྨ་རྣམ་པར་གནོན་པ་ལ་
ཕྱག་འཚལ་ལོ། །དེ་བཞིན་ག་ཤེགས་པ་དགྲ་བཅོམ་པ་ཡང་དག་པར་
རྫོགས་པའི་སངས་རྒྱས་རིན་པོ་ཆེའི་པདྨ་ལ་རབ་ཏུ་བཞུགས་པ་རི་དབང་གི་
རྒྱལ་པོ་ལ་ཕྱག་འཚལ་ལོ། །དེ་དག་ལ་སོགས་པ་ཕྱོགས་བཅུའི་འཇིག་རྟེན་
གྱི་ཁམས་ཐམས་ཅད་ན་དེ་བཞིན་ག་ཤེགས་པ་དགྲ་བཅོམ་པ་ཡང་དག་པར་
རྫོགས་པའི་སངས་རྒྱས་བཅོམ་ལྡན་འདས་གང་ཇི་སྙེད་ཅིག་བཞུགས་ཏེ་
འཚོ་ཞིང་གཤེགས་པའི་སངས་རྒྱས་བཅོམ་ལྡན་འདས་དེ་དག་ཐམས་ཅད་
བདག་ལ་དགོངས་སུ་གསོལ། བདག་གིས་སྐྱེ་བ་འདི་དང་། སྐྱེ་བ་ཐོག་མ

To the *Infinite Splendor*, I pay homage.

To the *Glorious Light*, I pay homage.

To the *Glorious One Without Sorrow*, I pay homage.

To the *Son of Nondesire*, I pay homage.

To the *Glory of Flowers*, I pay homage.

To the *Thus-Gone Clearly Knowing through the Play of Pure Radiance*, I pay homage.

To the *Thus-Gone Clearly Knowing through the Play of Lotus Radiance*, I pay homage.

To the *Glory of Wealth*, I pay homage.

To the *Glory of Vigilance*, I pay homage.

To the *Renowned Glorious Name*, I pay homage.

To the *King of the Victory Banner that crowns the Sovereign*, I pay homage.

To the *Glorious One Who Fully Subdues*, I pay homage.

To the *Perfect Victor in Battle*, I pay homage.

To the *One Gone Beyond Through Complete Victory*, I pay homage.

To the *Glorious Array Eternally Illuminating*, I pay homage.

To the *Lotus Jewel Who Fully Subdues*, I pay homage.

To the *Thus-Gone*, Conqueror of the enemy, perfect Buddha who dwells on a lotus jewel, King of the Sovereign Mount Meru, I pay homage.

དང་མཐའ་མ་མཉེས་པ་ནས། འཁོར་བ་ན་འཁོར་བའི་སྐྱེ་གནས་ཐམས་
ཅད་དུ་སྔིག་པའི་ལས་བགྱིས་པ་དང་། བགྱིད་དུ་སྩལ་བ་དང་། བགྱིས་པ་ལ་
རྗེས་སུ་ཡི་རང་བའམ། མཆོད་རྟེན་གྱི་དཀོར་རམ། དགེ་འདུན་གྱི་དཀོར་
རམ། ཕྱོགས་བཅུའི་དགེ་འདུན་གྱི་དཀོར་འཕྲོགས་པ་དང་། འཕྲོག་ཏུ་སྩལ་
བ་དང་། འཕྲོག་པ་ལ་རྗེས་སུ་ཡི་རང་བའམ། མཚམས་མ་མཉེས་པ་ལྔའི་
ལས་བགྱིས་པ་དང་། བགྱིད་དུ་སྩལ་བ་དང་། བགྱིས་པ་ལ་རྗེས་སུ་ཡི་རང་
བའམ། མི་དགེ་བ་བཅུའི་ལས་ཀྱི་ལམ་ཡང་དག་པར་བླངས་པ་ལ་ཞུགས་
པ་དང་། འཇུག་ཏུ་སྩལ་བ་དང་། འཇུག་པ་ལ་རྗེས་སུ་ཡི་རང་བའམ། ལས་
ཀྱི་སྒྲིབ་པ་གང་གིས་བསྒྲིབས་ནས། བདག་སེམས་ཅན་དམྱལ་བར་མཆི་
བའམ། དུད་འགྲོའི་སྐྱེ་གནས་སུ་མཆི་བའམ། ཡི་དྭགས་ཀྱི་ཡུལ་དུ་མཆི་
བའམ། ཡུལ་མཐའ་འཁོབ་ཏུ་སྐྱེ་བའམ། ཀླུ་ཀློར་སྐྱེ་བའམ། ལྷ་ཚེ་རིང་པོ་
རྣམས་སུ་སྐྱེ་བའམ། དབང་པོ་མ་ཚང་བར་འགྱུར་བའམ། ལྟ་བ་ལོག་པར་
འཛིན་པར་འགྱུར་བའམ། སངས་རྒྱས་འབྱུང་བ་ལ་མཉེས་པར་མི་བགྱིད་
པར་འགྱུར་བའི་ལས་ཀྱི་སྒྲིབ་པ་གང་ལགས་པ་དེ་དག་ཐམས་ཅད་སངས་
རྒྱས་བཅོམ་ལྡན་འདས་ཡེ་ཤེས་སུ་གྱུར་པ། སྤྱན་དུ་གྱུར་པ། དཔང་དུ་གྱུར་
པ། ཚད་མར་གྱུར་པ། མཁྱེན་པ། གཟིགས་པ། དེ་དག་གི་སྤྱན་སྔར་
མཐོལ་ལོ་འཆགས་སོ། །མི་འཆབ་བོ། མི་སྦེད་དོ། སླན་ཆད་ཀྱང་གཅོད་

To these and to all the Thus-Gone, the victors over the enemy, the perfect Buddhas, the conquerors, the holders, the transcendent Ones who dwell and live in all the worlds of the universe extending in the ten directions, to all these conquering Buddhas, holders, and transcendent Ones, I request that they pay attention to me.

During this life and lives that had neither beginning nor limit, in all the realms of existence of samsara that I have traveled through, I have accomplished negative acts; I have made others accomplish them, and rejoiced at causing others to accomplish them. I have stolen properties belonging to stupas, to the sangha, and properties of the sangha in the ten directions; I have made others steal them, and have rejoiced at causing others to steal them. I have committed the five acts with immediate consequences, I have made others commit them, and I have rejoiced at causing others to commit them. I have fully engaged the path of the ten harmful acts, I have led others to engage it, and rejoiced at causing others to engage it. Covered by these various karmic veils, I will go to the hells, I will go to the animal realms, I will go to the hungry ghosts realms, I will be born in places far from the Dharma, I will be born as a barbarian, I will be born among the gods of long life, I will not

ཅིང་སྐྱོབ་པར་བགྱིད་ལགས་སོ། །སངས་རྒྱས་བཅོམ་ལྡན་འདས་དེ་དག་
ཐམས་ཅད་བདག་ལ་དགོངས་སུ་གསོལ། བདག་གིས་སྐྱེ་བ་འདི་དང་སྐྱེ་བ་
ཐོག་མ་དང་མཐའ་མ་མ་མཆིས་པ་ནས། འཁོར་བ་ན་འཁོར་བའི་སྐྱེ་བ་
གཞན་དག་ཏུ་སྐྱིན་པ་ཐ་ན་དུད་འགྲོའི་སྐྱེ་གནས་སུ་སྐྱེས་པ་ལ་ཟས་ཁམ་
གཅིག་ཙམ་བསྩལ་བའི་དགེ་བའི་རྩ་བ་གང་ལགས་པ་དང་། བདག་གིས་
ཚུལ་ཁྲིམས་བསྲུངས་པའི་དགེ་བའི་རྩ་བ་གང་ལགས་པ་དང་། བདག་གིས་
ཚངས་པར་སྤྱོད་པ་ལ་གནས་པའི་དགེ་བའི་རྩ་བ་གང་ལགས་པ་དང་།
བདག་གིས་སེམས་ཅན་ཡོངས་སུ་སྨིན་པར་བགྱིས་པའི་དགེ་བའི་རྩ་བ་གང་
ལགས་པ་དང་། བདག་གིས་བྱང་ཆུབ་མཆོག་ཏུ་སེམས་བསྐྱེད་པའི་དགེ་
བའི་རྩ་བ་གང་ལགས་པ་དང་། བདག་གིས་བླ་ན་མེད་པའི་ཡེ་ཤེས་ཀྱི་དགེ་
བའི་རྩ་བ་གང་ལགས་པ་དེ་དག་ཐམས་ཅད་གཅིག་ཏུ་བསྡུས་ཤིང་བཟླུམས་
ཏེ། བསྡོམས་ནས་བླ་ན་མ་མཆིས་པ་དང་། གོང་ན་མ་མཆིས་པ་དང་། གོང་
མའི་ཡང་གོང་མ་བླ་མའི་ཡང་བླ་མར་ཡོངས་སུ་བསྔོ་བས། བླ་ན་མེད་པ་
ཡང་དག་པར་རྫོགས་པའི་བྱང་ཆུབ་ཏུ་ཡོངས་སུ་བསྔོ་བར་བགྱིའོ། །ཇི་ལྟར་
འདས་པའི་སངས་རྒྱས་བཅོམ་ལྡན་འདས་རྣམས་ཀྱིས་ཡོངས་སུ་བསྔོས་པ་
དང་། ཇི་ལྟར་མ་བྱོན་པའི་སངས་རྒྱས་བཅོམ་ལྡན་འདས་རྣམས་ཀྱིས་
ཡོངས་སུ་བསྔོ་བར་འགྱུར་བ་དང་། ཇི་ལྟར་ད་ལྟར་བྱུང་བའི་སངས་རྒྱས་

have all sense faculties, I will follow false views, I will not know to rejoice at the coming of a Buddha. All the veils coming from these acts, in the presence of the conquering Buddhas, Holders, and transcendent Ones, who have wisdom, who have vision, who are witnesses, who are truth, who know, who see, I acknowledge them, I do not conceal them, I do not hide them, and I promise to abstain from committing these acts from this time forward.

Conquering Buddhas, Holders, and Transcendent Ones, I request your attention. During this life and during lives that had neither beginning nor limit, in all the realms of existence of samsara that I have traveled through, all the sources of virtues that I have obtained from giving, whether it is only a mouthful of food to a being born in the animal realm, all the sources of virtue that I have obtained from the observance of ethic, all the sources of virtue that I have obtained through keeping pure conduct, all the sources of virtue that I have obtained from my own acts to make beings fully ripen, all the sources of virtue that I have obtained from generating sublime Bodhicitta, all the sources of virtue that I have obtained from unsurpassable wisdom, having gathered them, having brought them together, having accumulated them, I dedicate them to the unsurpassable, to the

བཅོམ་ལྡན་འདས་རྣམས་ཀྱིས་ཡོངས་སུ་བསྔོ་བར་མཛད་པ་དེ་བཞིན་དུ། བདག་གིས་ཀྱང་ཡོངས་སུ་བསྔོ་བར་བགྱིའོ། །སྡིག་པ་ཐམས་ཅད་ནི་སོ་སོར་བཤགས་སོ། །བསོད་ནམས་ཐམས་ཅད་ལ་རྗེས་སུ་ཡི་རང་ངོ་། །སངས་རྒྱས་ཐམས་ཅད་ལ་བསྐུལ་ཞིང་གསོལ་བ་འདེབས་སོ། །བདག་གིས་བླ་ན་མེད་པ་ཡེ་ཤེས་ཀྱི་མཆོག་དམ་པ་ཐོབ་པར་གྱུར་ཅིག །མི་མཆོག་རྒྱལ་བ་གང་དག་ད་ལྟར་བཞུགས་པ་དང་། གང་དག་འདས་པ་དག་དང་དེ་བཞིན་གང་མ་བྱོན། །ཡོན་ཏན་བསྔགས་པ་མཐའ་ཡས་རྒྱ་མཚོ་འདྲ་ཀུན་ལ། །ཐལ་མོ་སྦྱར་བར་བགྱིས་ཏེ་སྐྱབས་སུ་ཉེ་བར་མཆིའོ། །

highest of the highest, to the best of the best, I completely dedicate them to the supreme and perfect Awakening. In the same way as the conquering Buddhas, Holders, and Transcendent Ones of the past have accomplished perfectly their dedication, in the same way as the conquering Buddhas, holders, and transcendent Ones who have not yet come will accomplish perfectly their dedication, and in the same way as the conquering Buddhas, Holders, and Transcendent Ones of the present now perfectly accomplish their dedication, in the same way, I also accomplish the dedication perfectly.

I repent all negative acts, I rejoice in all merits, I address my exhortation and prayer to all Buddhas. May I obtain the unsurpassable, sublime, and holy wisdom. Whoever are the sublime human beings, the victors who live now, whoever are those who have come and even those who will come, I praise their qualities. In front of them all like a limitless ocean, I join my hands, and completely place myself under their protection.

The Thirty-five Buddhas

བཅོམ་ལྡན་འདས་དེ་བཞིན་གཤེགས་པ་དགྲ་བཅོམ་པ་ཡང་དག་པར་
རྫོགས་པའི་སངས་རྒྱས་ཤཱ་ཀྱ་ཐུབ་པ།

Shakyamuni, the Very Perfect Buddha,
the Conqueror, the Holder, the Transcendent One,
the Thus-Gone, the Victor of the enemies.

Diamond Essence

Vajragarbha

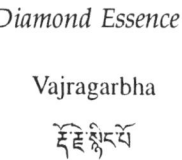

Jewel radiating Light

Ratnaprabhasambhava

King of Sovereign Nagas

Nageshvara

ཀླུ་དབང་གི་རྒྱལ་པོ་

Heroes' Leader

Virasena

དཔའ་བོའི་སྡེ་

Glorious Joy

Shrinanda

དཔལ་དགྱེས་

Fire Jewel

Ratnagni

རིན་ཆེན་མེ་

Moon Light Jewel

Ratnachandraprabha

རིན་ཆེན་ཟླ་འོད།

Meaningful Vision

Amoghadarshin

མཐོང་བ་དོན་ཡོད།

109

Moon Jewel

Ratnachandra

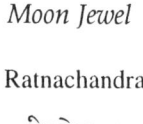
རིན་ཆེན་ཟླ་བ་

Immaculate One

Vimala

དྲི་མ་མེད་པ་

Glorious Gift

Shridatta

དཔལ་བྱིན

Pure One

Brahma

ཚངས་པ

Purity Gift

Brahmadatta

ཚངས་པས་བྱིན

Water God

Varuna

ཆུ་ལྷ

Water Gods' God

Varunadeva

རྒྱ་མཚོའི་ལྷ

Glorious Goodness

Bhadrashri

དཔལ་བཟང་

Glorious Sandalwood

Chandanashri

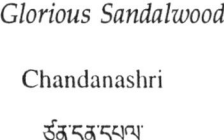

Infinite Splendor

Anantaujas

གཟི་བརྗིད་མཐའ་ཡས

Glorious Light

Prabhasashri

འོད་དཔལ་

Painless Glory

Ashokashri

མྱ་ངན་མེད་པའི་དཔལ་

115

Nondesire Son

Narayana

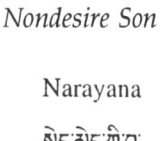

Flowers' Glory

Kusumashri

སྨེ་ཏོག་དཔལ་

Radiant Purity

Brahmajyotis

ཚངས་པའི་འོད་ཟེར་

Radiant Lotus

Padmajyotis

པདྨའི་འོད་ཟེར་

Wealth Glory

Dhanashri

ནོར་དཔལ་

Vigilance Glory

Smirtishri

དྲན་པའི་དཔལ་

*The Very Famous
Glorious Name*

Suparikirtitanamashri

མཚན་དཔལ་ཤིན་ཏུ་ཡོངས་གྲགས།

*King of the Banner
crowning the Sovereign*

Indraketuvijya

དབང་པོའི་ཏོག་གི་རྒྱལ་མཚན་གྱི་རྒྱལ་པོ་

*Glorious One who
totally subdues everything*

Suvikrantashri

ཤིན་ཏུ་རྣམ་པར་གནོན་པའི་དཔལ་

*The Perfect Victor
in the Battle*

Yuddhajaya

གཡུལ་ལས་ཤིན་ཏུ་རྣམ་པར་རྒྱལ་བ་

The Thus-Gone because of Complete Victory

Vikrantagami

རྣམ་པར་གནོན་པས་གཤེགས་པ་

Glorious Disposition eternally Illuminating

Samantavabhasavyuhashri

ཀུན་ནས་སྣང་བ་བཀོད་པའི་དཔལ་

Lotus Jewel

Ratnapadma

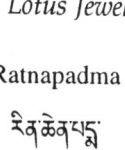
རིན་ཆེན་པད།

King of the Sovereign Mountain

Shailendraraja

རི་དབང་གི་རྒྱལ་པོ

SMALL GLOSSARY

AWAKENING: State of Buddhahood.

BEINGS: There are six classes of beings: gods, demigods, human beings, animals, hungry ghosts, and hell beings.

BUDDHA: One who has awakened. A person, as the historical Buddha Sakyamuni. In Tibetan, *Sangyay*. *Sang* means purified from the conflicting emotions, duality, and ignorance; *gyay* means that the infinite potential of qualities of a being is awakened.

BUDDHAHOOD: Awakened state characterized by wisdom (as knowledge of the true nature of phenomena and their manifestation in the three times), compassion for every being, and power to help all beings.

COMPASSION: Aspiration to liberate all beings from suffering and cause of suffering.

CONFLICTING EMOTIONS: Desire-attachment, hatred-aversion, ignorance or mental dullness, jealousy, pride, and so on.

DHARMA: Buddha's teachings or the spiritual path.

DHARMAKAYA: Absolute Body, designating a state beyond any spacial or temporal determination; corresponds to emptiness.

KAGYUPA: One of the four great schools of Tibetan Buddhism. The other ones are Gelugpa, Nyingma, and Sakya schools. The Kagyu lineage originates with Marpa the Translator in the 11th century.

KARMA: The law of karma describes the process of cause and effect. It is a three-phase process:
- an act leaves an imprint in the mind of the one who acts (cause).
- this act is stored in the potential of consciousness and is slowly ripening.
- this process is actualized in a particular form of suffering or joy (result).

LAMA (Tibetan): Guru (Sanskrit). A spiritual teacher.

LOVE: Aspiration to bring happiness to all beings.

NIRMANAKAYA: Body of Emanation; appears as human or other forms to guide ordinary beings.

SAMBHOGAKAYA: Body of Perfect Enjoyment, it appears to guide beings in the Pure Lands.

SAMSARA: Cycle of conditioned existence in which each being is born and dies. It is characterized by suffering, ignorance, impermanence, and illusion.

SANGHA: Community of Buddhist practitioners. One distinguishes ordinary sangha from the Noble Sangha which is composed of those who have attained the bodhisattva levels.

STUPA: Monument or sacred object symbolizing the mind of the Buddhas and which spreads their spiritual energies.

SUTRA (Sanskrit): Text of the exoteric teachings of the Buddha.

SVABHAVIKAKAYA: Body of Essence Itself, unity of the three first Bodies (Dharmakaya, Nirmanakaya, and Sambhogakaya).

TAKING REFUGE: Placing oneself under the protection of the Buddha, Dharma, and Sangha (the Three Jewels). In the Vajrayana, one takes also Refuge in the Three Roots, lamas, yidams, and dharma protectors.

TANTRA: Text of the esoteric teachings of the Buddha which is related to a deity.

TEN DIRECTIONS: North, South, East, West, four intermediate positions, zenith, and nadir.

THREE TIMES: The past, present, and future.

VAJRAYANA: Path of Buddhism also called "Diamond vehicle" referring to the part of the Buddha's teachings written in texts of an esoteric nature called tantras. It uses recitation of mantras, visualizations of deities and works with the subtle winds or energies.

Index